SECOND EDITION

TOUCHSTONE

WORKBOOK 1A

MICHAEL MCCARTHY
JEANNE MCCARTEN
HELEN SANDIFORD

CAMBRIDGE
UNIVERSITY PRESS

University Printing House, Cambridge CB2 8BS, United Kingdom

One Liberty Plaza, 20th Floor, New York, NY 10006, USA

477 Williamstown Road, Port Melbourne, VIC 3207, Australia

314–321, 3rd Floor, Plot 3, Splendor Forum, Jasola District Centre, New Delhi – 110025, India

79 Anson Road, #06–04/06, Singapore 079906

Cambridge University Press is part of the University of Cambridge.

It furthers the University's mission by disseminating knowledge in the pursuit of education, learning and research at the highest international levels of excellence.

www.cambridge.org
Information on this title: www.cambridge.org/9781107670716

© Cambridge University Press 2005, 2014

This publication is in copyright. Subject to statutory exception and to the provisions of relevant collective licensing agreements, no reproduction of any part may take place without the written permission of Cambridge University Press.

First published 2005
Second Edition 2014

20 19 18 17 16 15 14 13 12 11 10 9 8 7 6 5 4 3 2

Printed in the United Kingdom by Latimer Trend

A catalog record for this publication is available from the British Library.

ISBN 978-1-107-67987-0 Student's Book
ISBN 978-1-107-62792-5 Student's Book A
ISBN 978-1-107-65345-0 Student's Book B
ISBN 978-1-107-63933-1 Workbook
ISBN 978-1-107-67071-6 Workbook A
ISBN 978-1-107-69125-4 Workbook B
ISBN 978-1-107-68330-3 Full Contact
ISBN 978-1-107-66769-3 Full Contact A
ISBN 978-1-107-61366-9 Full Contact B
ISBN 978-1-107-64223-2 Teacher's Edition with Assessment Audio CD/CD-ROM
ISBN 978-1-107-61414-7 Class Audio CDs (4)

Additional resources for this publication at www.cambridge.org/touchstone2

Cambridge University Press has no responsibility for the persistence or accuracy of URLs for external or third-party internet websites referred to in this publication, and does not guarantee that any content on such websites is, or will remain, accurate or appropriate. Information regarding prices, travel timetables, and other factual information given in this work is correct at the time of first printing but Cambridge University Press does not guarantee the accuracy of such information thereafter.

Contents

1 All about you 2
2 In class 10
3 Favorite people 18
4 Everyday life 26
5 Free time 34
6 Neighborhoods 42

All about you

UNIT 1

Lesson A Hello and good-bye

1 Meetings and greetings

Vocabulary **A** Complete the conversations. Choose and write the best response.

1. A Hello.
   B *Hi.* _____
   (a.) Hi.
   b. Good-bye.

2. A Hi. I'm Ted.
   B _____
   a. Hi, I'm Lucille. Nice to meet you.
   b. See you next week.

3. A How are you?
   B _____
   a. I'm Kyle.
   b. I'm fine, thanks.

4. A Good-bye.
   B _____
   a. See you later.
   b. Thanks.

5. A Good night.
   B _____
   a. Hello.
   b. Bye. See you tomorrow.

6. A Hi. How are you?
   B _____
   a. Good, thanks. How are you?
   b. Have a nice day.

Vocabulary **B** **Complete the conversations with the expressions in the box.**

Good night.	✓Hello.	How are you?	Nice to meet you.
Have a good evening.	Hi.	I'm fine	See you

1. **Jack** *Hello.* I'm Jack.
   Anna _____ I'm Anna.
   Jack _____

2. **Sonia** Hi, Julie. How are you?
   Julie Good. _____
   Sonia _____, thanks.

3. **Mike** _____
   Koji Thanks. You too.

4. **Joan** _____
   Mary Bye. _____ tomorrow.

C **Complete the instant message.**

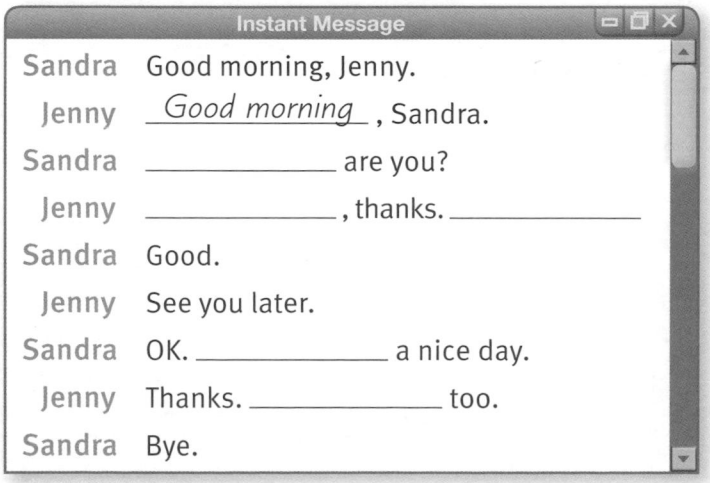

Instant Message

Sandra Good morning, Jenny.
Jenny *Good morning*, Sandra.
Sandra _____ are you?
Jenny _____, thanks. _____
Sandra Good.
Jenny See you later.
Sandra OK. _____ a nice day.
Jenny Thanks. _____ too.
Sandra Bye.

1 My name's Eva.

Vocabulary **Complete the conversation.**

A Good morning.
B Good morning.
A How are you?
B I'm fine.
A What's your *name*?
B Eva Salazar.
A How do you spell your _____ name?
B It's S-A-L-A-Z-A-R.
A And what's your _____ name?
B Eva.
A OK. How do you _____ *Eva*?
B E-V-A.
A And are you Ms., Miss, or _____ ?
B Ms.
A Thank you. Have a nice day.
B Thanks. You too.

2 Your personal information

Vocabulary **Complete the form. Use your own information.**

Touchstone English Club

NAME: _____
First Middle Last

☐ single ☐ married

CLASS: _____

ROOM: _____

TEACHER: _____

3 Are we in the same class?

Grammar **A Complete the conversation. Write *am* or *are*. Use contractions *'m* or *'re* where possible.**

Receptionist Hello. ___Are___ you here for an English class?
Mi-Young Yes, I _____ . I'm Mi-Young.
Receptionist Mi-Young Lee? You _____ in Class C.
Mi-Young Thank you.
Sergio Hi. _____ I in Class C, too? I'm Sergio.
Receptionist Yes, you _____ .
Sergio So we _____ in the same class.
Receptionist Wait. _____ you Sergio Rodrigues?
Sergio No, I _____ not. I'm Sergio Lopes.
Receptionist Oh, you _____ in Class D. You _____ not in the same class.

B Complete the conversation.

David Hi. _____ _____ Julia Kim?
Leti No, _____ _____ . I'm Leticia Martinez, but everyone calls me Leti.
David Hi, Leti. I'm David. Nice to meet you.
Leti _____ _____ here for a dance class?
David Yes, _____ _____ . _____ _____ in the same class?
Leti Yes, _____ _____ . We're in Class A.

4 About you

Grammar **Answer the questions. Use your own information.**

1. Are you in an English class?

_____

2. Are you in a French class?

_____

3. How are you today?

_____

4. Are you and your friends in the same English class?

_____

5. Are you married?

_____

1 What's the number?

Vocabulary **A** Write the numbers.

0	1	2	3	4	5
zero	_____	_____	_____	_____	_____
	6	7	8	9	10
	_____	_____	_____	_____	_____

B Complete the crossword puzzle.

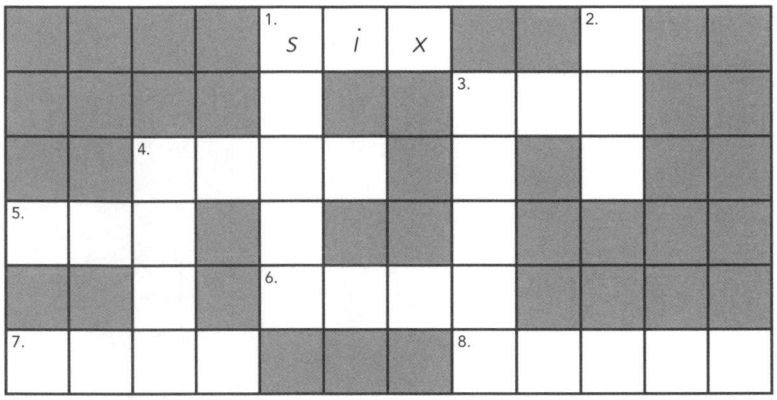

Across

1. two × three = *six*
3. two + eight = _____
4. ten ÷ two = _____
5. six – four = _____
6. three + six = _____
7. five × zero = _____
8. six + two = _____

Down

1. ten – three = _____
2. eight – seven = _____
3. eight – five = _____
4. two × two = _____

2 What's the word?

Vocabulary The letters spell a word. Write each letter in the correct box below to see the word.

1. C	3. H	5. N	7. E	9. U
2. O	4. O	6. T	8. S	10. T

ten	four	nine	one	three	eight	six	two	five	seven
			C						

3 Here's your membership card.

Grammar **Look at Mark's student ID card. Write his answers in the conversation.**

Lee Hello. Are you a member of the club?

Mark No, I'm not.

Lee OK. Well, here's an application form. So, what's your last name?

Mark *It's Brokaw.* **or** *Brokaw.* **or** *My last name's Brokaw.*

Lee Thank you. And your first name?

Mark _____

Lee What's your middle initial, please?

Mark _____

Lee And what's your email address?

Mark _____

Lee And your phone number?

Mark _____

Lee Are you an English student?

Mark _____

Lee What's your teacher's name?

Mark _____

Lee Thank you. Here's your membership card. Have a nice day.

4 About you

Grammar and vocabulary **Write questions with *What's* and the words given. Then answer the questions with your own information.**

1. A *What's your name?*
   (your name)
   B _____

2. A _____
   (your cell phone number)
   B _____

3. A _____
   (your email address)
   B _____

4. A _____
   (your English teacher's name)
   B _____

Lesson D Are you here for the concert?

1 Good evening.

Conversation strategies

Complete the conversations with the expressions in the box. Use each expression only one time.

Good evening.	✓ Hi	How about you?	How are you doing?	Thank you.	Yes
Pretty good.	Hello.	Nice to meet you.	Good-bye.	thanks.	Yeah

1. **Sam** Hi, Ali.
   Ali *Hi*, Sam. _____
   Sam Good, thanks. How about you?
   Ali _____
   Sam Am I late?
   Ali _____, you are, but it's OK.
   Sam Good. By the way, here's your book.
   Ali Oh, _____

2. **Joe** Good evening.
   Clerk _____ What's your name, please?
   Joe Joe Johnson.
   Clerk Oh, yes. Mr. Johnson. Your room number is 10A. Here's your key.
   Joe _____

3. **Sally** Hello. My name's Sally.
   Kate _____ I'm Kate. _____
   Are you here on business?
   Sally _____, I am. _____
   Kate No, I'm on vacation.
   Sally Nice. Oh, here's a taxi. _____
   Kate Bye.

2 How are you doing?

Conversation strategies

A Rewrite the conversation. Use less formal expressions for the underlined words.

A Hello. How are you?	A *Hi. How are you doing?*
B I'm fine, thank you. How are you?	B _____
A I'm fine. Are you a student here?	A _____
B Yes, I am. How about you?	B _____
A Yes, me too.	A _____
B What's the email address here?	
A It's goodschool1@cup.org.	
B Thank you. Good-bye.	B _____
A Good-bye.	A _____

B Number the lines of the conversation in the correct order. Then write the conversation.

____ Hi.	A *Hello.*
____ Yeah, me too.	B _____
____ OK.	A _____
____ Are you here for the concert?	B _____
____ How are you doing?	A _____
1 Hello.	B _____
____ Yeah, I am. How about you?	A _____

Unit 1 Progress chart

What can you do? Mark the boxes. ✓ = I can . . . ? = I need to review how to . . .	To review, go back to these pages in the Student's Book.
Grammar	
☐ make statements with *I'm (not), you're (not),* and *we're (not).*	2, 4, and 5
☐ ask questions with *Are you . . . ?*	5
☐ ask questions with *What's . . . ?*	4, 6, and 7
☐ give answers with *It's . . . .*	6 and 7
Vocabulary	
☐ say *hello* and *good-bye* in at least 4 different ways.	1, 2, and 3
☐ talk about names in English.	2 and 4
☐ use numbers 0–10.	6
Conversation strategies	
☐ use *How about you?*	8
☐ use everyday expressions in more formal and less formal situations.	9

In class

UNIT 2

Lesson A Classmates

1 Where is everybody today?

Grammar **A** Look at the pictures. Complete the sentences.

1. Bill *'s* _____ at the gym. *He's* not at home.

2. Jon and Karen *are* at home. _____ not in class.

3. Sun-Yee _____ in the cafeteria. _____ late.

4. David _____ on vacation. _____ asleep.

5. Kate and Tess _____ in class. _____ not at the library.

6. Carmen _____ at work. _____ not sick.

B Complete the questions about the people in part A. Then answer the questions.

1. A *Is* Bill at work?
   B *No, he's not.*
2. A _____ Jon and Karen at home?
   B _____
3. A _____ Sun-Yee at the gym?
   B _____
4. A _____ David asleep?
   B _____
5. A _____ Kate and Tess on vacation?
   B _____
6. A _____ Carmen at work?
   B _____

2 Absent classmates

Grammar **Complete the conversation with the verb *be*. Use contractions where possible. Add *not* where necessary.**

Silvia Hi. How ___are___ you?
Jason Good, thanks. How about you?
Silvia Pretty good. _____ Dave here?
Jason No, he _____ _____.
I think he _____ sick.
Silvia Oh. _____ he at home?
Jason I don't know.
Silvia How about Jenny and Paula?
_____ they here?
Jason No, they _____ _____. They _____ on vacation. I think they _____ in Miami.
Silvia Look! Dave _____ not sick. He _____ over there. He _____ just late again!

3 About you

Grammar and vocabulary **Complete the questions with the names of your friends and classmates. Then answer the questions.**

1. A Is ___Paul___ at home?
   B ___Yes, he is.___
2. A Are _____ and _____ at work?
   B _____
3. A Is _____ in class today?
   B _____
4. A Are _____ and _____ on vacation?
   B _____
5. A Are _____ and _____ in your English class?
   B _____
6. A Is _____ sick today?
   B _____
7. A Is _____ at the library?
   B _____
8. A Are _____ and _____ asleep?
   B _____

Lesson B What's in your bag?

1 Everyday things

Vocabulary | **Label the things in the pictures. Use *a* or *an* where necessary.**

1. *a pen*
2. _____
3. _____
4. _____
5. _____
6. _____
7. _____
8. _____
9. _____
10. _____
11. _____
12. _____
13. _____
14. _____
15. _____
16. _____

2 What are these things?

Grammar and vocabulary | **Write sentences about the pictures.**

1. *This is a bag.*

2. *These are pens.*

3. _____

4. _____

5. _____

6. _____

7. _____

8. _____

3 Asking about things

Grammar **Complete the conversations. Use the words in the box.**

Is	it	it's	these	they're	this	What
Is	it's	these	they	they're	this	✓What's

1. **Clerk** You're in Room 102.
   Ms. Simms Thanks. *What's* this?
   Clerk Oh, _____ your room key.
   Ms. Simms OK. Thank you.
   Clerk And _____ is your membership card for the fitness club.

2. **Erica** What's _____ ? _____ it a smartphone?
   Jim No, _____ not. It's a GPS.
   Erica Oh.
   Jim _____ are these?
   Erica I think _____ watches.

3. **Bob** What are _____ ?
   Jill Oh, no! I think _____ my jeans.
   Bob Oh, I'm sorry. Are _____ new?
   Jill Yeah. Oh, look. _____ this your wallet?
   Bob Yes, _____ is.
   Jill Oh, no! And _____ are your credit cards!

Lesson C In the classroom

1 Classroom things

Vocabulary **A** Write the words under the pictures. Use *a* or *some*.

1. *a board*

2. *some posters*

3. _____

4. _____

5. _____

6. _____

7. _____

8. _____

9. _____

10. _____

11. _____

12. _____

B Circle the words from part A in the puzzle. Look in these directions (→ ↓). Which word is *not* in the puzzle?

T	V	C	Q	U	A	B	L	A	M	A	B
W	E	H	A	S	I	P	U	Y	A	Z	O
A	C	A	L	E	N	D	A	R	P	H	A
G	O	I	H	K	O	B	Z	O	E	O	R
I	P	R	P	E	D	L	F	L	T	E	D
W	A	S	T	E	B	A	S	K	E	T	I
R	K	T	O	R	R	J	O	O	M	U	M
O	C	U	O	S	J	E	C	D	E	S	K
N	L	L	G	T	O	R	X	I	T	J	A
C	O	M	P	U	T	E	R	O	T	D	S
M	C	A	S	M	P	O	S	T	E	R	S
A	K	S	C	I	S	S	O	R	S	A	R

2 A classroom

Grammar and vocabulary

A Look at the picture. Complete the sentences. Use the words in the box.

in | in front of | in front of | next to | ✓on | on | on | under

1. The workbooks are ___on___ the table.
2. The calendar is _____ the wastebasket.
3. The computer is _____ the teacher's desk.
4. The map is _____ the window.
5. The students' papers are _____ the wall.
6. The teacher's desk is _____ the board.
7. The scissors are _____ the teacher's desk.
8. The table is _____ the chairs.

B Write the questions about the classroom in part A.

1. A ___Where's the teacher's desk?___
   B It's in front of the board.
2. A _____
   B It's next to the window.
3. A _____
   B They're on the table.
4. A _____
   B They're under the teacher's desk.
5. A _____
   B They're on the wall.
6. A _____
   B It's in the wastebasket.

3 Missing apostrophes

Grammar

Put apostrophes (') in the correct places in the questions. Then answer the questions.

1. What's on the wall in your classroom? _____
2. What are your friends names? _____
3. Whats your English teachers name? _____
4. Wheres your teacher now? _____

Lesson D How do you spell it?

1 Questions, questions

Conversation strategies **Complete the conversations. Use the expressions in the box.**

✓Excuse me	Thanks anyway.	Sure.	Here you go.	Thanks.
Can I borrow	You're welcome.	please	How do you spell	Sorry.
What's the word for this in English?				

1. **Callie** *Excuse me*, Bob.
   Bob Yeah?
   Callie _____ your English book?
   Bob Sure. Now, where is it?
   Callie Um . . . it's right in front of you.
   Bob Oh, yeah. _____
   Callie Thanks.
   Bob _____

2. **Ruby** Can I borrow your cell phone,
   _____?
   Millie _____ Oh, wait.
   It's not in my bag. I think it's at home.
   _____
   Ruby That's OK. _____
   Millie Sure. . . . _____
   Ruby In English, the word is *umbrella*.
   Millie Umbrella? Thanks.
   Ruby Sure.

3. **Yuri** _____ *computers*?
   Dan C-O-M-P-U-T-E-R-S.
   Yuri _____
   Dan Sure.
   Yuri And how do you spell *television*?
   Dan T-V.
   Yuri Very funny!

2 Scrambled conversations

Conversation strategies

Number the lines of the conversations in the correct order. Then write the conversations.

1. _____ I'm sorry. A *You're late.*
   _____1_____ You're late. B _____
   _____ That's OK. A _____

2. _____ Sure. A _____
   _____ Thank you. B _____
   _____ Can I borrow your pen, please? A _____
   _____ You're welcome. B _____

3. _____ I don't know. A _____
   _____ That's OK. Thanks anyway. B _____
   _____ That's OK. What about this? A _____
   _____ I'm sorry. I don't know. B _____
   _____ What's the word for this? A _____

Unit 2 Progress chart

What can you do? Mark the boxes. ✓ = I can . . . ? = I need to review how to . . .	To review, go back to these pages in the Student's Book.
Grammar	
☐ make statements with *he's (not)*, *she's (not)*, and *they're (not)*.	12 and 13
☐ ask questions with *Is he . . . ?*, *Is she . . . ?*, and *Are they . . . ?*	13
☐ use *a* or *an*.	14
☐ make nouns plural with *-s*, *-es*, or *-ies*.	15
☐ use *this* with singular nouns and *these* with plural nouns.	14 and 15
☐ ask questions with *Where . . . ?*	17
☐ use *'s* and *s'* to show possession.	17
Vocabulary	
☐ name at least 8 things students take to class.	14 and 15
☐ name at least 12 classroom items.	16 and 17
☐ say where things are in the classroom.	16 and 17
Conversation strategies	
☐ ask for help in class.	18
☐ use common responses to *Thank you* and *I'm sorry*.	19

Favorite people

UNIT 3

Lesson A Celebrities

1 Favorites

Vocabulary **A** **Unscramble the letters. Write the words.**

1. rgiens s*inger*
2. ctrao a_____
3. rtweir w_____
4. maet t_____
5. ralype p_____
6. dnab b_____
7. prsot s_____
8. naf f_____
9. ivome m_____
10. rtiats a_____

B **Complete the crossword puzzle with the words in part A.**

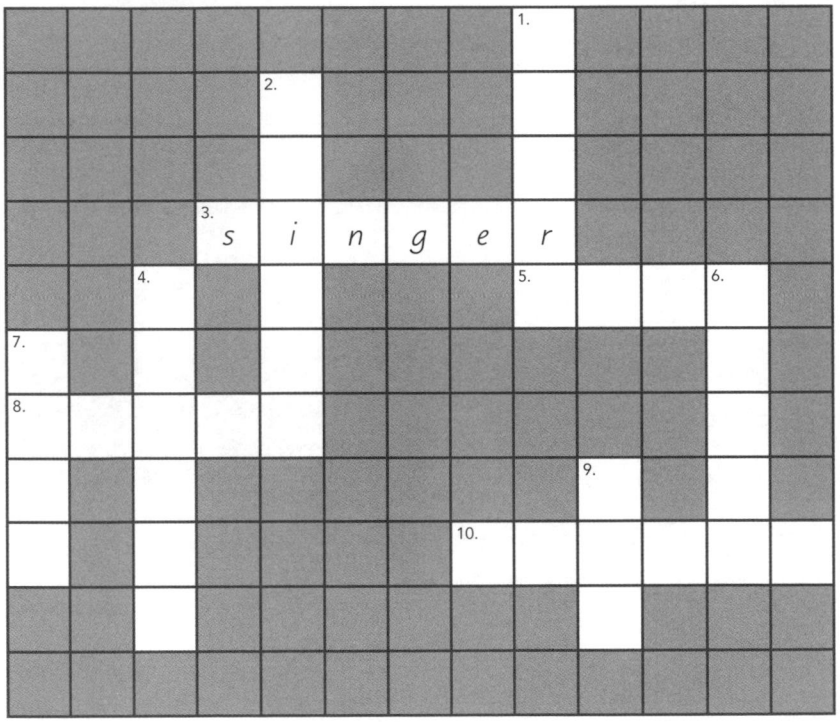

Across

3. Adele is an amazing _____.
5. Our favorite soccer _____ is Manchester United.
8. Hugh Jackman is a great _____.
10. Ronaldo is a famous soccer _____.

Down

1. Soccer is a _____.
2. J.K. Rowling is a famous _____.
4. Who's your favorite _____?
6. This _____ is exciting.
7. My favorite _____ is Coldplay.
9. Brian is a _____ of the Giants.

2 She's my favorite singer.

Grammar **Look at the pictures. Complete the sentences.**

1. "She's my favorite singer. Her new album is great."

2. "_____ Jama fans. Jama is _____ favorite band."

3. "_____ a great writer. _____ new book is really good."

4. "_____ favorite movie is *The Aliens*. What's _____ favorite movie?"

5. "_____ my favorite actors. I think _____ movies are very good."

6. "Cassandra Coe is my teacher. _____ a great artist. _____ pictures are amazing."

3 They're great!

Grammar **Complete the conversation with the verb *be*. Use contractions where possible.**

Alicia I love this new Bruno Mars album. He 's my favorite singer.

Norah Yeah. I ____ a big fan of his, too. His voice _____ amazing. His songs _____ great.

Alicia Yeah. So, what's your favorite band?

Norah Maroon 5. They ____ great.

Alicia Yes, they _____ very talented. Adam Levine _____ really good looking. He ____ my favorite.

Lesson B People we know

1 What are they like?

Vocabulary **Look at the pictures. Complete the sentences. Use the words in the box.**

busy	fun	lazy	✓quiet	smart	tired
friendly	interesting	outgoing	shy	strict	

1. She's *quiet* and _____.

2. He's _____.

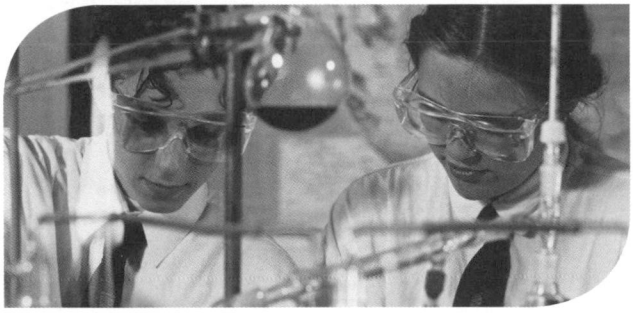

3. They're _____.

4. She's _____.

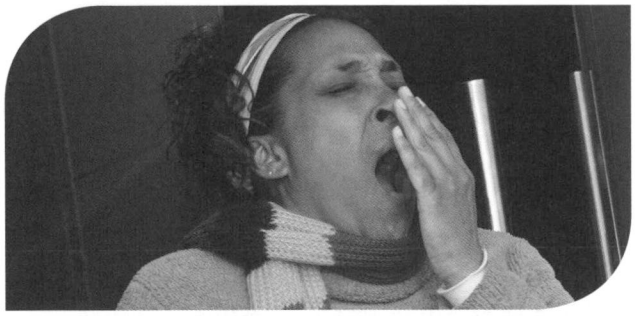

5. She's _____.

6. He's _____.

7. He's not very _____ or _____.

8. They're _____. She's _____.

2 What's new?

Grammar **Complete the conversation with the verb *be*. Use contractions where possible. Add *not* where necessary.**

Carrie Sorry. *Am* I late?

Josh No, you _____ _____. You _____ fine.

Carrie Good. So, what's new? _____ you busy at work?

Josh Yes, I _____. Our boss _____ sick, so he _____ _____ at work.

Carrie Oh, really?

Josh So, how about you? What _____ your new neighbors like? _____ they nice?

Carrie Yes, they _____. They _____ OK. They _____ very quiet.

Josh _____ they students?

Carrie No, they _____ _____. The guy _____ a writer.

Josh A writer? What about the woman? _____ she a writer, too?

Carrie No, she _____ _____. She _____ _____ a writer – she _____ a teacher. At our school!

3 Make it negative.

Grammar **Rewrite the sentences in the negative form. Use contractions where possible.**

1. My neighbors are very nice. *My neighbors aren't very nice.*
2. My best friend is a student. _____
3. I'm very shy. _____
4. The students in my class are very smart. _____
5. My English class is easy. _____
6. My teacher is very quiet. _____

4 About you

Grammar and vocabulary **Complete the questions. Then write short answers. Add more information.**

1. *Are* you outgoing? *Yes, I am. I'm very outgoing.*
   or *No, I'm not. I'm not outgoing.*
2. _____ your best friend lazy? _____
3. _____ your English class hard? _____
4. _____ your friends smart? _____
5. _____ your teacher fun? _____
6. _____ your classmates nice? _____
7. _____ you tired today? _____
8. _____ you and your friends busy after class? _____

1 Who's who?

Vocabulary **Use the family tree to complete the sentences about this family.**

1. David is Paul's *son* .
2. John is Katy's _____ .
3. Katy is Paul's _____ .
4. Josh, David, and Emily are Paul and Katy's _____ .
5. Emily is Josh's _____ .
6. Josh is David's _____ .
7. John and Catherine are Katy's _____ .
8. Katy is Josh's _____ .
9. John is Catherine's _____ .
10. Emily is Katy's _____ .
11. Catherine is David's _____ .
12. John is Emily's _____ .
13. Susan is David's _____ .
14. Bill is Josh's _____ .
15. Robert is Emily's _____ .

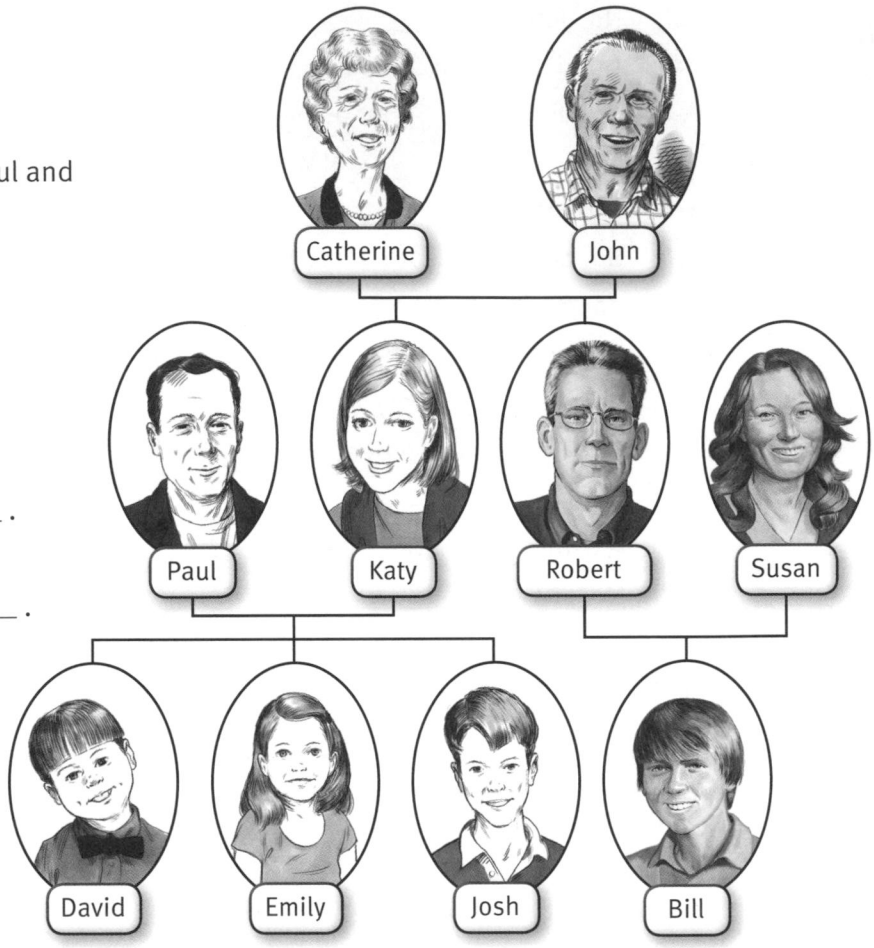

2 What's the number?

Vocabulary **Write the numbers.**

65 — 1. *sixty-five*

11 — 2. _____

24 — 3. _____

15 — 4. _____

16 — 5. _____

91 — 6. _____

56 — 7. _____

77 — 8. _____

3 How about your children?

Grammar and vocabulary **Complete the conversations. Write the full questions.**

1. A How / your parents?

   How are your parents?

   B They're fine. Thanks. How / your mom?

   _____

   A She's good. She's on vacation right now.

2. A What / your sisters' names?

   _____

   B Beth and Kate. My brother's name is Pete.

   A Pete? Oh, how old / he?

   _____

   B He's 21.

3. A Who / this?

   _____

   B Oh, it's my aunt.

4. A My cousins are really fun.

   B Yeah? How old / they?

   _____

   A They're my age.

5. A Where / your family today?

   _____

   B At home. How about your family?

   A They're at home, too.

6. A Where / you from?

   _____

   B Well, my parents are from Italy originally.

   A Really? Where / your parents from in Italy?

   _____

   B They're from Rome.

4 A famous family

Grammar **Read part of a phone interview with an actor. Then write questions for the answers.**

Interviewer Hello, Kate. How are you?
Kate Hi. I'm fine, thanks.
Interviewer Kate, I love your movies.
Kate Thank you.
Interviewer Now, about your family . . . who's your mother?
Kate Gwen Russell – the artist. And Kevin Russell is my father.
Interviewer Yes, they're famous! What are your parents like at home?
Kate Oh, Dad's fun and outgoing. And Mom's very smart!
Interviewer And, Kate, what's your favorite band?
Kate Imagine Dragons. They're amazing. . . .

1. *How is Kate?*
   She's fine.
2. _____
   Her mother is Gwen Russell.
3. _____
   Her father is fun and outgoing. Her mother is very smart.
4. _____
   Her favorite band is Imagine Dragons.

Lesson D A songwriter? Really?

1 New neighbors and co-workers

Conversation strategies **Complete the conversations with the questions in the box.**

How old is she?	Where is she from?	✓What are they like?	An actor? Is she good?
From Chile?	Are they friendly?	Are they good?	Where are they from?

1. **Ming** Who are they?
   Jim Oh, they're my new neighbors.
   Ming Your neighbors? *What are they like?*
   Jim Interesting. Very interesting. They're in a rock band.
   Ming A rock band? _____
   Jim They're from New York.
   Ming Wow! _____
   Jim No, they're not.
   Ming Uh-oh. _____
   Jim Oh, very. Their friends are always here!

2. **Carlos** Who's she?
   Kim Her name's Angie.
   Carlos Angie? _____
   Kim I don't know exactly. I think she's from Chile.
   Carlos _____ Really? What's she like?
   Kim She's outgoing and fun.
   Carlos Really? _____
   Kim I'm not sure. Maybe 24 or 25.
   Carlos Oh. What's her job? Is she a server here?
   Kim Well, yes. But she's an actor, too.
   Carlos _____
   Kim Yeah, she's a good actor but not a great server.

2 Really? I'm surprised!

Conversation strategies **Write responses to show you are interested or surprised. Then ask a question.**

1. My grandmother's name is Banu. *Really? What's she like?*
2. My brother is a singer in a band. _____
3. My grandfather is a tennis player. _____
4. I'm from Alaska. _____
5. My mother is a Spanish teacher. _____
6. My new job is hard work. _____
7. My sister is an artist. _____
8. My last name is Oh. _____

Unit 3 Progress chart

	What can you do? Mark the boxes. ✓ = I can . . . ? = I need to review how to . . .	To review, go back to these pages in the Student's Book.
Grammar	☐ use *my*, *your*, *his*, *her*, *our*, and *their*.	22 and 23
	☐ make statements with *be*.	22 and 23
	☐ ask *yes-no* questions with *be*.	24 and 25
	☐ make negative statements with *be*.	24 and 25
	☐ ask information questions with *be*.	26 and 27
Vocabulary	☐ name at least 8 words to describe people's personalities.	24 and 25
	☐ name at least 12 family words.	26 and 27
	☐ say numbers 10–101.	26
Conversation strategies	☐ show interest by repeating information and asking questions.	28
	☐ use *Really?* to show interest or surprise.	29

Everyday life

UNIT 4

Lesson A In the morning

1 What's Kathy's morning like?

Grammar and vocabulary

A **Complete the sentences about Kathy's morning. Use the correct form of the verbs in the box.**

check	exercise	✓get up	play
eat	get up	listen	read

1. Kathy *gets up* early. Her son _____ late.

2. She _____ before work. Her son _____ games.

3. She _____ to the radio in the car.

4. She and her co-workers _____ breakfast together.

5. Kathy _____ her email right after breakfast.

6. Her boss _____ the newspaper at work.

B **Rewrite the sentences in the negative form. Use contractions where possible.**

1. Kathy's son gets up early. *Kathy's son doesn't get up early.*
2. Kathy checks her email before breakfast. _____
3. Kathy and her son talk a lot in the morning. _____
4. Kathy's son does his homework. _____
5. Kathy and her boss eat breakfast together. _____
6. Kathy's boss plays computer games. _____

2 Guess what!

Grammar **Complete Peter's email with the correct form of the verbs.**

New Message

To: Samir22@cup.com
From: PeterJ@cup.com
Subject: New Job

Hi!

Guess what! I *have* (have) a new job – in a coffee shop. It's hard work. I _____ (get up) early, and I _____ (work) late. But the coffee is good.

My boss is nice. He's French, and he _____ (study) English at night. He _____ (do) his homework in the coffee shop. I _____ (help) him sometimes. He's quiet, and he _____ (not / talk) a lot. He _____ (listen) to the radio and _____ (sing), but we _____ (not / like) the same music. He _____ (like) coffee, too. We both _____ (have) four cups of coffee every day!

Write soon!

Peter

3 Typical morning activities

Grammar and vocabulary **A What are typical morning activities? Match the verbs with the words and expressions.**

1. do *d*	a. to the radio
2. study ____	b. (my) email or messages
3. check ____	c. a car
4. listen ____	✓d. (my) homework
5. drive ____	e. on the Internet
6. play ____	f. English
7. read ____	g. games on the computer
8. go ____	h. a book

B Write true sentences about your morning routine. Use the verbs in part A.

1. *I don't do my homework in the morning.*
2. _____
3. _____
4. _____
5. _____
6. _____
7. _____
8. _____

1 What's fun? What's not?

Vocabulary **A** Which routine activities are fun for you? Complete the charts. Add your own ideas.

check email	do the laundry	go shopping	take a class
clean the house	eat snacks	make phone calls	text friends
do homework	get up early	✓ play sports	watch TV

Fun!	
play sports	

Not fun!	

B Write the days of the week in the date book. Then write one thing you do each day.

S*unday*: *I go shopping on Sundays.*
M_____: _____
T_____: _____
W_____: _____
Th_____: _____
F_____: _____
S_____: _____

2 About you 1

Grammar and vocabulary Use time expressions to write one thing you do and one thing you don't do.

1. on the weekends *I clean the house on the weekends.*
   I don't go to work on the weekends.
2. after work / class _____
   _____
3. every day _____
   _____
4. on Saturdays _____
   _____
5. in the afternoons _____
   _____
6. at night _____
   _____

3 What's your week like?

Grammar **Complete the conversation with the correct form of the verbs.**

Cecilia What's your week like, Eduardo? ___Do___ (Do / Does) you ___go___ (go / goes) to work every day?

Eduardo Well, no, I _____ (don't / doesn't). I work at home on Fridays.

Cecilia Really? What about on the weekends? _____ (Do / Does) you _____ (work / works) then, too?

Eduardo Yes, I _____ (do / does). But I don't like it. What about you? _____ (Do / Does) you and your husband _____ (go / goes) to work every day?

Cecilia Yes, we _____ (do / does). But just Monday to Friday. We _____ (clean / cleans) the house on the weekends. Oh, and we _____ (go / goes) to soccer games.

Eduardo Oh. _____ (Do / Does) your son _____ (play / plays) soccer?

Cecilia Yes, he _____ (do / does). He's on the school team. _____ (Do / Does) your son _____ (play / plays) any sports?

Eduardo No, he _____ (don't / doesn't). He plays games on his computer.

4 About you 2

Grammar and vocabulary **Complete the questions. Then write answers with your own information.**

1. A ___Do___ you ___take___ a class at night?
   B *Yes, I do. I take a Spanish class on Monday evenings.*
2. A _____ your father _____ the laundry on weekends?
   B _____
3. A _____ you and your friends _____ shopping on Saturdays?
   B _____
4. A _____ your friends _____ their email before breakfast?
   B _____
5. A _____ your mother _____ the news on the Internet every day?
   B _____

Do you work out every day?

1 Saying more than *yes* or *no*

Conversation strategies

A Complete the conversation. Use the sentences in the box.

I work part-time in the cafeteria.	It's fun, and the people are nice.
Just Mondays and Wednesdays.	I'm an English student.
✓ I'm new here, and I'm late.	I go there Mondays after work. It's great!

Mike Hi. Are you OK? You look lost.

Yumi Hello. Where's Room 106? Do you know?
I'm new here, and I'm late.

Mike Yeah. It's right over there, next to the cafeteria.

Yumi Thanks. So, do you work here?

Mike Yes, I do. _____

Yumi Do you like the job?

Mike Yeah, I do. _____

Yumi That's good. Do you work here every day?

Mike Well, no. _____
I go to class on Tuesdays and Thursdays.

Yumi Oh. So you're a student, too?

Mike Yeah. _____

Yumi Really? I'm an English student, too. Do you belong to the English Club?

Mike Yes, I do. _____

Yumi Oh. Well, thanks a lot. And see you at English Club!

Mike Great!

B Read the completed conversation again. Then read the sentences below. Check (✓) *T* (true) or *F* (false).

	T	F
1. Mike and Yumi are friends.	☐	☑
2. Mike works in the cafeteria.	☐	☐
3. Mike is a new student.	☐	☐
4. Mike works Tuesdays and Thursdays.	☐	☐
5. Mike likes his part-time job.	☐	☐
6. Yumi and Mike are English students.	☐	☐
7. Mike belongs to the English Club.	☐	☐

2 About you

Conversation strategies

Unscramble the questions. Then answer the questions. Write more than *yes* or *no*. Use *Well* if you need to.

1. live / you / around / Do / here ?

   Do you live around here?

2. from / originally / you / here / Are ?

3. a / full-time / you / Are / student ?

4. have / you / brothers / Do / sisters / or ?

5. you / work / the / on / weekends / Do ?

6. Do / your / every day / text / friends / you ?

7. get up / day / you / Do / every / early ?

8. grandparents / Do / with / your / live / you ?

1 Watching TV

Reading **A** **What do you think average Americans do after work and school? Check (✓) three boxes.**

- ☐ spend time with family
- ☐ go out with friends
- ☐ read
- ☐ go out to dinner
- ☐ watch TV
- ☐ go shopping

B **Read the article. Check your answers in part A.**

After WORK and SCHOOL

Do Americans go out every night after work and have fun? Maybe the answer is surprising, but no, they don't. They don't usually go out with friends in the evening, and they don't go out to dinner or go shopping. So what do they do? Well, about 90% of Americans stay at home in the evening to relax. In fact, it's their favorite activity. They read, watch TV, and spend time with their families.

So what about young people? Well, they spend a lot of time at home, too. American high school students study about six hours a week and watch TV for about 15 hours a week.

Most Americans also have a hobby and do fun, interesting things like play sports or music. Americans stay home a lot, but they stay busy, too!

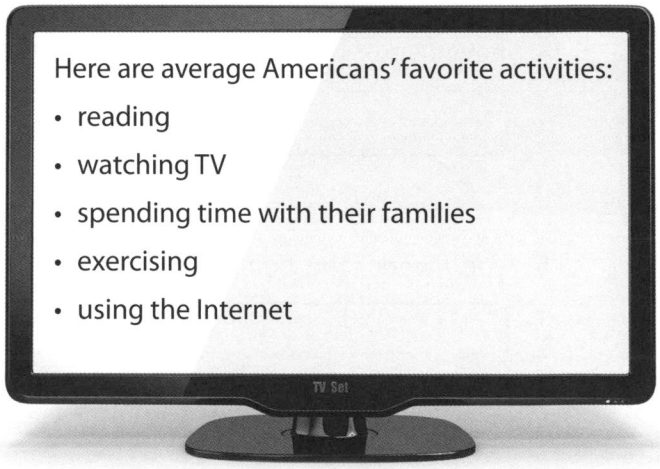

C **Read the article again. Then correct these false sentences.**

1. Americans go out with friends every night after work.
   Americans don't usually go out with friends in the evening.
2. After work, Americans usually go shopping.
   _____
3. American high school students usually study for three hours a night.
   _____
4. American high school students don't watch TV.
   _____
5. The average American doesn't have a hobby.
   _____

2 Weekends

Writing **A Read the email messages. Then rewrite Joe's message. Use capital letters and periods.**

New Message

Hi Joe,
Are you busy on weekends?
I am. On Friday nights, I go to a club in Miami. On Saturdays, I sleep late. In the evening, I watch TV. On Sundays, I study. Do you study on the weekends?
Ian

New Message

hi ian,
yes, i have busy weekends on friday nights, i visit my family downtown on saturdays,
i take a spanish class at grove college on sundays, i play soccer i don't study on weekends – i don't have time
joe

New Message

Hi Ian,

_____
_____
_____
_____
_____
_____
_____
_____

B What do you do on weekends? Write an email to a friend about your weekend activities.

New Message

Hi _____,

_____
_____
_____
_____
_____
_____

Unit 4 Progress chart

	What can you do? Mark the boxes. ✓ = I can . . . ? = I need to review how to . . .	To review, go back to these pages in the Student's Book.
Grammar	☐ make simple present statements. ☐ ask simple present *yes-no* questions and give short answers.	34 and 35 36 and 37
Vocabulary	☐ name at least 12 new verbs for routine activities. ☐ name the days of the week. ☐ name at least 8 time expressions with the simple present.	34, 35, 36, and 37 36 37
Conversation strategies	☐ answer questions with more than *yes* or *no*. ☐ use *Well* to get time to think of an answer.	38 and 39 39
Writing	☐ use capital letters and periods.	41

Free time

UNIT 5

Lesson A Going out

1 In your free time

Vocabulary **How often do you do these things? Complete the chart with the free-time activities in the box. Add your own ideas.**

✓eat out	go out with friends	go to a club	go to the gym	play a sport
go on the Internet	go shopping	go to a movie	have dinner with family	text family

every day	three or four times a week	once or twice a week	once or twice a month
		eat out	

2 Craig's busy schedule

Grammar and vocabulary **A Read Craig's weekly planner. Are the sentences below true or false? Write *T* (true) or *F* (false). Then correct the false sentences.**

WEEKLY PLANNER

SUNDAY	MONDAY	TUESDAY	WEDNESDAY	THURSDAY	FRIDAY	SATURDAY
5 morning: *do the laundry!!* evening: *dinner with Mom and Dad*	**6** morning: *classes* afternoon: *go shopping*	**7** morning: *go to the gym!* afternoon: *library*	**8** morning: *classes* afternoon: *guitar lesson*	**9** morning: *go to the gym!* evening: *dinner with Sandra*	**10** morning: *classes* evening: *movie with Jim*	**11** morning: *clean the house!!* afternoon: *tennis with Bob* evening: *club with Bill*

1. He goes out with friends ~~every evening~~ *three evenings a week*. *F*
2. He goes to the library every day. ____
3. He goes shopping once a week. ____
4. He takes guitar lessons on Wednesday mornings. ____
5. He plays tennis twice a week. ____
6. He does the laundry three times a week. ____
7. He sees his parents on the weekends. ____
8. He cleans the house on Saturday mornings. ____

Grammar **B Now answer these questions about Craig's schedule.**

1. How often does he go to the gym? *He goes to the gym twice a week.*
2. When does he have classes? _____
3. How often does he go to a club? _____
4. What does he do on Thursday evenings? _____
5. When does he go to the movies? _____
6. What does he do on Saturday afternoons? _____
7. Who does he play tennis with? _____
8. Where does he go on Saturday evenings? _____

3 About you

Grammar and vocabulary **Write questions for a friend. Then answer your friend's questions.**

1. You *Where do you go after class?*
   (go after class)
   Friend I meet some friends and go to a restaurant for dinner. How about you?
   You _____

2. You _____
   (text your friends)
   Friend Every day. But I don't text before breakfast. How about you?
   You _____

3. You _____
   (do in your free time at home)
   Friend I rent a movie, or I just relax in front of the TV with a friend. How about you?
   You _____

4. You _____
   (go on the weekends)
   Friend I go to a restaurant or club. How about you?
   You _____

5. You _____
   (go out with)
   Friend Oh, friends from school. How about you?
   You _____

Lesson B TV shows

1 How often?

Grammar **A** **Write the frequency adverbs in order in the chart below.**

✓always hardly ever never often sometimes usually

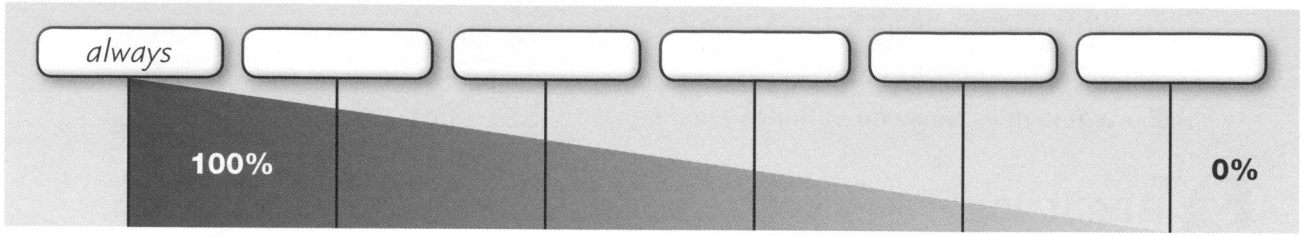

B **Answer the questions. Write true sentences using frequency adverbs.**

What's something you . . .

1. hardly ever do before school or work? *I hardly ever check my email before school.*
2. always do in the morning? _____
3. sometimes do after school or work? _____
4. never do during dinner? _____
5. often do in the evening? _____
6. usually do on Saturdays? _____

2 What kinds of TV shows do you know?

Vocabulary **A** **Look at the pictures. Circle the correct type of TV show.**

1. soap opera / the news

2. talk show / cartoon

3. sitcom / the news

4. cartoon / game show

5. documentary / talk show

6. talk show / cartoon

7. sitcom / reality show

8. the news / game show

B Circle the kinds of TV shows from part A in the puzzle. Look in these directions (→↓).

T	C	S	I	T	C	O	M	E	T	I	S
E	A	O	E	D	H	P	O	R	H	I	H
L	R	E	A	L	I	T	Y	S	H	O	W
K	T	A	L	K	S	H	O	W	U	P	O
S	O	A	P	O	P	E	R	A	E	E	U
D	O	C	U	M	E	N	T	A	R	Y	N
A	N	O	O	T	H	E	J	E	I	W	S
Y	T	E	A	I	U	W	D	O	C	T	V
Y	C	G	A	M	E	S	H	O	W	L	Y

3 About you

Grammar and vocabulary

Answer the questions. Give two pieces of your own information in each answer.

1. Do you ever watch soap operas? *Yes, I usually watch soap operas in the afternoons. I love the stories.*
2. What sitcoms do you hardly ever watch? _____
3. How often do you watch documentaries? _____
4. What talk shows do you like? _____
5. When do you usually watch the news? _____
6. How often do you watch reality shows? _____

Lesson C Do you go straight home?

1 Asking questions in two ways

Conversation strategies **Complete the conversations with the questions in the box.**

Do you like French?	I mean, do you belong to any clubs?
✓ Do you do anything special?	I mean, do you know a nice place?
Do you play baseball?	I mean, do you go every day?

1. **Lisa** What do you do after work?
   Do you do anything special?
   Debbie Well, I go to the gym.
   Lisa Really? How often do you go?
   _____
   Debbie No, not every day. I go Mondays, Wednesdays, and Thursdays.

2. **Howard** Do you know the restaurants around here?
   _____
   Mary Well, I often go to a little place on Main Street. What kind of food do you like?
   _____
   Howard Yes, I do. I love French food.

3. **Paul** What do you do after school?
   _____
   Tom Well, yeah. I'm in the Sports Club.
   Paul Really? What do you play?
   _____
   Tom Well, no. We watch baseball on TV!
   Paul Oh.

2 Questions, questions

Conversation strategies **Write a second question for each question below. Then write true answers.**

1. What's your teacher like?
   I mean, is she nice?
   Yes, she's very nice. She's friendly.
2. How often do you have English class?
   _____
   _____
3. How do you get to school / work?
   _____
   _____
4. What do you do for fun on the weekends?
   _____
   _____
5. Do you read a lot?
   _____
   _____
6. Do you ever go to clubs?
   _____
   _____

3 About you

Conversation strategies **Add frequency adverbs to make these sentences true for you. Then use *I mean*, and write more information.**

1. I *never* go to the gym. *I mean, I usually exercise at home.*
2. I _____ get home early. _____
3. I _____ see my friends during the week. _____
4. I _____ go on the Internet in the evening. _____
5. I _____ eat breakfast at school / work. _____
6. I _____ get up early. _____
7. I _____ eat out on Saturdays. _____
8. I _____ watch reality shows on TV. _____
9. I _____ go shopping on the weekends. _____
10. I _____ study English after dinner. _____

Lesson D Technology addicts

1 Paula's problem

Reading **A Read Paula's post to an online forum. How many hours does Paula spend online?**

☐ 3 or 4 hours ☐ 4 or 5 hours ☐ 8 or 9 hours

PaulaT18 posted 2 hours ago

I live with my parents and my two brothers. They say I hardly ever spend time with them. My parents say I spend too much time on my phone and in front of my computer, but I don't think that's true. I mean, I often get up early and check my messages, but we always eat breakfast together. I guess I sometimes text during breakfast, but I never call people then. After class, I listen to music on my phone, but I also do my homework. In the evening, I often log on to my social network to chat with friends. They're always online. Sometimes I watch a movie on my computer. I usually spend eight or nine hours online every day. I don't think it's a problem. What do you think?

B Read Paula's post again. Then answer the questions.

1. Who does Paula live with? *She lives with her parents and her two brothers.*
2. Is she a student? _____
3. When does she log on to her social network? _____
4. What does Paula use her phone and computer for? _____
5. What do you think? Does Paula have a problem? Why or why not? _____

2 I need some advice!

Writing **A Read José's post to an online forum. Complete it with *and* or *but*.**

José posted 2 hours ago

I think I have a problem. I don't have a computer at home, ___but___ I use a computer at school. I usually go to school early, _____ I check my email. I send email to my friends in other countries. I often go online for fun, _____ sometimes I study English on the computer. Then on the weekends, I go to school _____ write papers for class (on the computer). Do I spend too much time at school?

B Write a post for an online forum about a problem you have. Write about a problem below, or use your own idea.

"I watch too much TV." "I go shopping too much." "I work too much."
"I stay home too much." "I talk on my cell phone too much." "I study too much."

_____
_____
_____
_____
_____
_____

Unit 5 Progress chart

What can you do? Mark the boxes. ✓ = I can . . . ? = I need to review how to . . .	To review, go back to these pages in the Student's Book.
Grammar	
☐ ask simple present information questions.	44 and 45
☐ use time expressions like *once a week*.	44 and 45
☐ use frequency adverbs like *sometimes*, *never*, etc.	46
Vocabulary	
☐ name at least 6 new free-time activities.	44 and 45
☐ name at least 6 kinds of TV shows.	47
☐ talk about likes and dislikes.	47
Conversation strategies	
☐ ask questions in 2 ways to be less direct.	48
☐ use *I mean* to repeat an idea and say more.	49
Writing	
☐ use *and* and *but* to link ideas.	51

Neighborhoods

UNIT 6

Lesson A Nice places

1 What's in the neighborhood?

Vocabulary **Label the places in the picture. Use the words in the box with *a / an* or *some*.**

✓apartment buildings	fast-food places	museum	park	restaurants	supermarket
club	movie theater	outdoor café	post office	stores	swimming pool

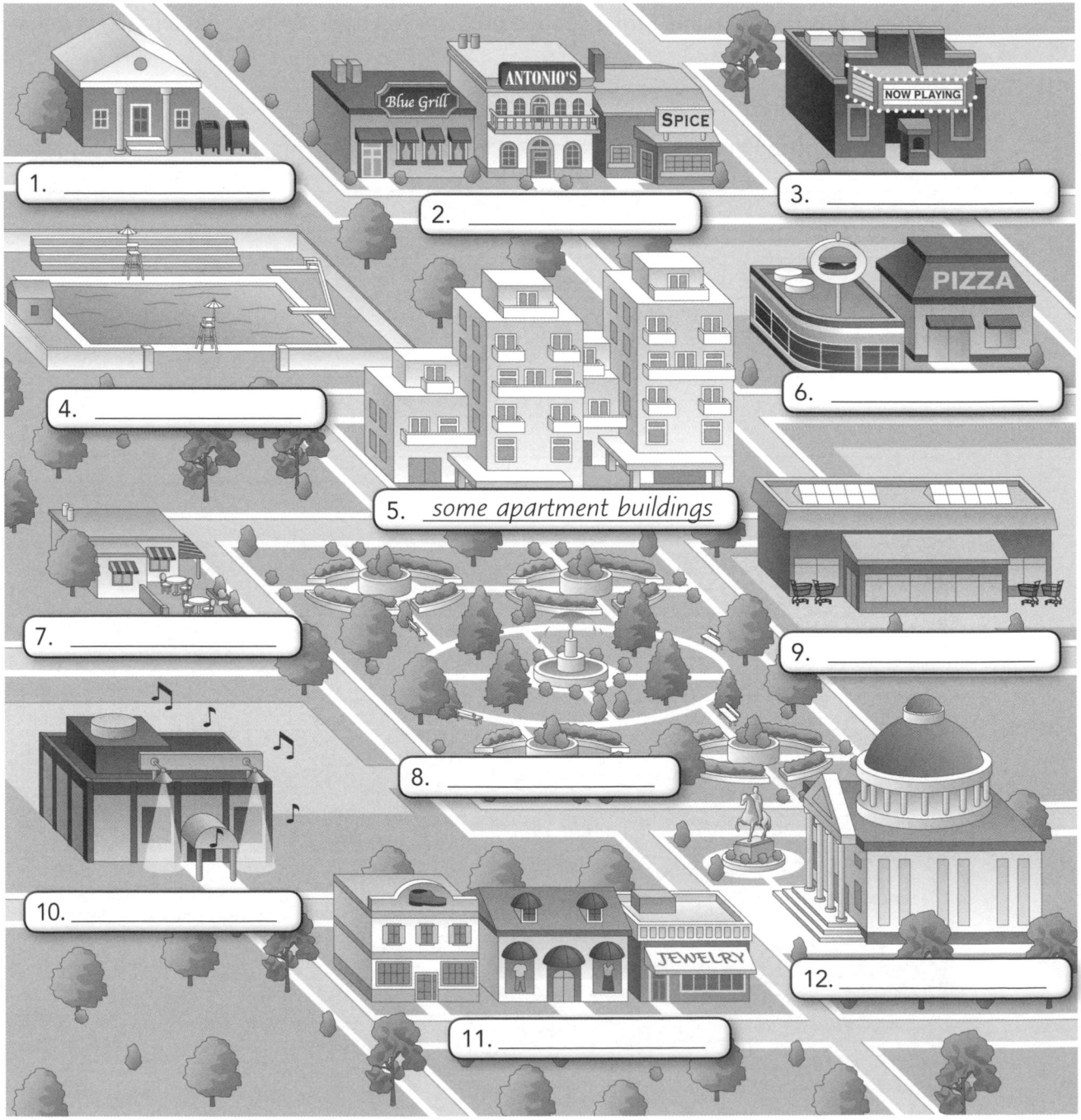

2 Can you find the opposites?

Vocabulary **Find six pairs of adjective opposites in the box. Write them in the chart below.**

bad	boring	expensive	interesting	noisy	quiet
big	cheap	good	✓new	✓old	small

new – old

3 That's not quite right!

Grammar **Look at the picture on page 42. Correct the sentences to describe the neighborhood.**

1. There's one cheap fast-food place. *There are a couple of cheap fast-food places.*
2. There are a couple of post offices. _____
3. There's a big stadium. _____
4. There are a couple of supermarkets. _____
5. There are some malls. _____
6. There's an apartment building. _____
7. There are no small stores. _____
8. There's an expensive restaurant. _____
9. There are a lot of beautiful parks. _____
10. There's no movie theater. _____

4 About you

Grammar and vocabulary **What's your neighborhood like? Complete the sentences with true information.**

1. There's a _____.
2. There are a lot of _____.
3. There are some _____.
4. There are a couple of _____.
5. There's no _____.
6. There are no _____.

Lesson B What time is it?

1 What's the time?

Vocabulary **A** **Write the times in words. Where there are two lines, write the times two ways.**

1. *It's twelve p.m.*
   It's noon.

2. _____
   _____

3. _____

4. _____

5. _____
   _____

6. _____
   _____

B **Read about Kayo's day. Write the times in numbers. Then number the sentences in the correct order.**

_____ Her bus comes at *7:55* (five to eight).

_____ She gets home at _____ (nine fifteen) and watches TV.

1 Kayo gets up at _____ (six twenty-five).

_____ She goes for lunch with her co-workers at _____ (noon).

_____ She starts work at _____ (eight forty-five).

_____ She meets her boyfriend at _____ (twenty five to six), and they have dinner.

_____ She eats breakfast at _____ (twenty after seven).

_____ She leaves work at _____ (ten after five).

_____ She goes to bed at _____ (ten thirty).

2 Let's do it!

Grammar **Complete the conversations. Write questions starting with *What time . . . ?* Use *Let's* to end each conversation with a suggestion.**

1. A I'm starving. Let's go to Burger Queen.
   B But it's late. *What time does it close?*
   A It closes around 11:00, I think. _____
   B Almost 10:00. _____

2. A There's a new reality show on TV tonight.
   B _____
   A Um, I think it starts at 8:00.
   B Well, I'm really tired. _____
   A I'm not sure. I think it ends at 9:30.
   B OK. _____

3. A Let's go to the gym on Saturday morning.
   B Sure. _____
   A Oh, it opens early. At 6:00. _____
   B I usually get up around 8:00 on Saturdays.
   A OK. _____

3 About you

Grammar and vocabulary **Unscramble the questions. Then write true answers.**

1. do / What time / get up / on weekdays / you ?
   A *What time do you get up on weekdays?*
   B _____

2. your family / have / What time / does / lunch / on Sundays ?
   A _____
   B _____

3. your English class / What time / start / does ?
   A _____
   B _____

4. What time / leave home / do / you / in the morning ?
   A _____
   B _____

5. stores / do / What time / in your neighborhood / open and close ?
   A _____
   B _____

Lesson C Me too!

1 Responses

Conversation strategies **Circle the two correct responses to each comment. Cross out the incorrect response.**

1. I think every neighborhood needs a park.
   a. ~~Me neither.~~
   b. Me too.
   c. Right.
2. We don't have a good fast-food place here.
   a. Yeah.
   b. Me too.
   c. I know.
3. I don't like the new restaurant.
   a. Yeah. I know.
   b. Me neither.
   c. Me too.
4. There are no good bookstores around here.
   a. I know.
   b. Me too.
   c. Right.
5. I like the new outdoor café downtown.
   a. Me neither.
   b. Me too.
   c. Right. It's good.
6. I love this neighborhood. It's so quiet.
   a. Right.
   b. Yeah, I know.
   c. Me neither.

2 What do they have in common?

Conversation strategies **Read the conversation. Are the sentences below true or false? Write *T* (true) or *F* (false).**

Glen What's your new neighborhood like?

Anna Oh, it's amazing. There are a lot of outdoor cafés and movie theaters and clubs. I go out a lot.

Glen Really? I hardly ever go out in my neighborhood. It's boring.

Anna Let's do something in my neighborhood this weekend. I'm free on Saturday.

Glen Me too.

Anna Well, there's a great jazz club near my apartment. I love jazz.

Glen Really? Me too!

Anna But let's have dinner at a café first. The food at the club is expensive, and I don't have a lot of money.

Glen Me neither. So, let's meet at 6:30 at your apartment.

1. Glen and Anna both like their neighborhoods. __F__
2. Glen and Anna both go out a lot in their neighborhoods. ____
3. Glen and Anna are both free on Saturday. ____
4. Glen and Anna both love jazz. ____
5. Glen and Anna both have a lot of money. ____

Help note

*Glen and Anna **both** love jazz. Glen loves jazz, **and** Anna loves jazz, **too**.*

3 Right. I know.

Conversation strategies **Circle the expression that is true about your neighborhood. Then show you agree. Respond with *Right* or *I know*.**

1. A **There are some** / **There are no** good restaurants in my neighborhood.
   B *I know.*
2. A My neighborhood **has** / **doesn't have** a lot of great stores.
   B _____
3. A I live in a **great** / **terrible** neighborhood.
   B _____
4. A We **need** / **don't need** a shopping mall around here.
   B _____

4 About you

Conversation strategies **Imagine you're talking to people from your neighborhood. Write true responses.**

1. I really like this neighborhood.
   Me too. I think it's great.
   or
   Really? I don't like it very much.
2. I don't eat out in this neighborhood.
   _____
3. I think the restaurants are very expensive here.
   _____
4. I don't know a lot of people around here.
   _____
5. I think our neighborhood is boring.
   _____
6. I think we need a couple of new stores in our neighborhood.
   _____

Lesson D A neighborhood guide

1 Free weekend events!

Reading **A** **Read about some local events on a website. Match the pictures with the events. Write the correct numbers next to the pictures.**

Downtown Weekend Section

* * * FREE EVENTS * * *

1. All Day Music Meet local bands, singers, and musicians at City Park this Sunday. Listen to great music, dance to pop songs, or take a music workshop and write your own song! The music starts at 3 p.m. and finishes at 11 p.m. Call Melissa at 555-9075 for more information.

2. Spring Food Festival Do you love food? Do you often eat out? Then come to the Parkview Food Festival. Eat some delicious food from 20 different restaurants around the neighborhood – all for FREE! *Saturday from 11:00 a.m. to 4:00 p.m. at Green Street Park.*

3. Outdoor Street Fair *Saturday and Sunday from 10:00 a.m. to 6:00 p.m. in front of the City Art Museum.* There are a lot of beautiful items for sale – books, art, photos, paintings, clothes, and more. Items for sale are just $2–$25. Coffee, sodas, and snacks are for sale, too!

4. Free Classes at the Neighborhood Center Do you want to take a class but don't have the time? Try a free one-hour class Monday through Friday this week. Learn:

- Art
- Spanish
- Music
- French
- Computers
- Yoga

Classes start at 10:00 a.m. and 2:00 p.m. Go to www.freeclass.cup.org for more information.

B **Read the website again. Then answer the questions. Check (✓) the correct events.**

Which events . . .	The concert	The food festival	The street fair	The free classes
1. have food?	☐	☑	☑	☐
2. are on Saturday?	☐	☐	☐	☐
3. have a website?	☐	☐	☐	☐
4. are during the day?	☐	☐	☐	☐
5. are at night?	☐	☐	☐	☐
6. are outdoors?	☐	☐	☐	☐

2 Make your own event.

Writing **A Complete the sentences with the prepositions in the box.**

at at at between for ✓from on through to

1. The event is *from* 6:00 _____ 10:00.
2. The event is _____ 8:00 p.m. _____ the stadium _____ Main Street.
3. Go to www.eventinfo.cup.org _____ more information, or call Jim _____ 555-7777.
4. Call _____ 12:00 p.m. and 5:00 p.m., Monday _____ Friday.

B Imagine you are planning an event. Answer the questions. Use the ideas in the boxes and your own ideas.

Events:	Places:
a play, an art exhibit, a concert, a sports event	the library, the museum, the park, the theater

1. What is the event? _____
2. When and where is it? _____
3. What time does it start and finish? _____
4. What's the cost of the event? Is it free? _____
5. What things are there to do at the event? _____
6. Where or how do people get more information? _____

C Write an ad for an event in your town or city. Give the event a name.

_____

_____

_____

Unit 6 Progress chart

	What can you do? Mark the boxes. ✓ = I can . . . ? = I need to review how to . . .	To review, go back to these pages in the Student's Book.
Grammar	☐ use *There's* and *There are* with singular and plural nouns.	54 and 55
	☐ use quantifiers *a lot of*, *some*, *a couple of*, and *no*.	54 and 55
	☐ use adjectives before nouns.	55
	☐ ask and answer questions about time.	56 and 57
	☐ make suggestions with *Let's*.	57
Vocabulary	☐ name at least 6 adjectives to describe places.	54 and 55
	☐ name at least 10 words for neighborhood places.	54 and 55
	☐ give times for events.	56 and 57
Conversation strategies	☐ answer *Me too* or *Me neither* to show I'm like someone.	58 and 59
	☐ answer *Right* or *I know* to agree.	59
Writing	☐ use prepositions *at*, *from*, *in*, *on*, and *to* with times, places, and days.	61

Illustration credits

Ken Batelman: 42 **Harry Briggs:** 15, 61 *(4 at bottom)*, 69 **Domninic Bugatto:** 8, 23, 27, 38, 59, 78 **Cambridge University Press:** 67 **Matt Collins:** 22, 54 **Chuck Gonzales:** 5, 11, 26, 45, 80 **Cheryl Hoffman:** 3, 24, 47, 61 *(2 at top)* **Jon Keegan:** 19, 51, 94, 95 **Frank Montagna:** 2, 13, 21, 53, 82, 83 **Greg White:** 7, 16, 37, 79 **Terry Wong:** 30, 46, 63, 74, 86 **Filip Yip:** 70

Photo credits

3 *(clockwise from top left)* ©Exactostock/SuperStock; ©Elea Dumas/Getty Images; ©MIXA/Getty Images; ©Thinkstock **4** ©Ryan McVay/Getty Images **7** ©wavebreakmedia/Shutterstock **10** *(clockwise from top left)* ©Andresr/Shutterstock; ©MTPA Stock/Masterfile; ©Spencer Grant/PhotoEdit; ©Jose Luiz Pelaez Inc./Corbis; ©Medioimages/Photodisc/Thinkstock; ©Terry Doyle/Getty Images **11** *(top to bottom)* ©Image Source/SuperStock; ©kurhan/Shutterstock **12** *(pen)* ©Phant/Shutterstock; *(potato chips)* ©Thinkstock; *(wallet)* ©AlexTois/Shutterstock; *(laptop)* ©Alex Staroseltsev/Shutterstock; *(umbrella)* ©K. Miri Photography/Shutterstock; *(bag)* ©Hemera Technologies/Thinkstock; *(glasses)* ©Ingvar Bjork/Shutterstock; *(keys)* ©SELEZNEV VALERY/Shutterstock; *(notebook)* ©zirconicusso/Shutterstock; *(smartphone)* ©Oleksiy Mark/Shutterstock; *(water bottle)* ©lucadp/Shutterstock; *(eraser)* ©GreenStockCreative/Shutterstock; *(watch)* ©Venus Angel/Shutterstock; ©Butterfly Hunter/Shutterstock; *(pencil)* ©Julia Ivantsova/Shutterstock; *(hand holding smartphone)* ©Thinkstock; *(hand holding water bottle)* ©DenisNata/Shutterstock; *(all others)* ©George Kerrigan **14** *(top row, left to right)* ©Rtimages/Shutterstock; ©Cambridge University Press; ©Thinkstock; ©Cambridge University Press *(middle row, left to right)* ©Ryan McVay/Thinkstock; ©Ryan McVay/Thinkstock; ©Thinkstock; ©Pixtal/age Fotostock *(bottom row, left to right)* ©Cambridge University Press; ©Cambridge University Press; ©Photodisc/Thinkstock; ©vovan/Shutterstock **19** ©Design Pics/SuperStock **20** *(clockwise from top left)* ©Exactostock/SuperStock; ©Exactostock/SuperStock; ©Mark Scott/Getty Images; ©Fancy Collection/SuperStock; ©Andreas Pollok/Getty Images; ©Ron Chapple/Getty Images; ©rSnapshotPhotos/Shutterstock; ©Peter Cade/Getty Images **28** ©Don Nichols/Getty Images **29** *(top to bottom)* ©Larry Dale Gordon/Getty Image; ©Punchstock **32** *(television)* ©Maxx-Studio/Shutterstock **35** *(top to bottom)* ©Darren Mower/Getty Images; ©Thinkstock **36** *(top row, left to right)* ©JOSE LUIS SALMERON Notimex/Newscom; ©The Everett Collection; ©The Everett Collection; ©Getty Images *(bottom row, left to right)* ©Lions Gate/courtesy Everett Collection; ©Eric Roberts/Corbis; ©Robert Voets/CBS via Getty Images; ©Ann Johansson/Corbis **40** ©violetblue/Shutterstock **43** *(left to right)* ©Maxx-Studio/Shutterstock; ©MariusdeGraf/Shutterstock **44** *(clockwise from top left)* ©Cambridge University Press; ©Artur Synenko/Shutterstock; ©Cambridge University Press; ©Cambridge University Press; ©Cambridge University Press; ©Cambridge University Press **45** ©Punchstock **47** ©Anders Blomqvist/Getty Images **48** *(left to right)* ©Ambient Images Inc./Alamy; ©Yellow Dog Productions/Getty Images; ©Spencer Grant/PhotoEdit; ©David Grossman/Imageworks **50** *(clockwise from top left)* ©Holly Harris/Getty Images; © Kwame Zikomo/SuperStock; © Jens Lucking/Getty Image; © Kaz Chiba/Getty Images; © Onoky/SuperStock; © I. Hatz/Masterfile **52** *(top row, all photos)* ©Cambridge University Press *(middle row, left to right)* ©Cambridge University Press; ©Rudy Umans/Shutterstock; ©JupiterImages *(bottom row, left to right)* ©JupiterImages; ©Cambridge University Press; ©Danilo Calilung/Corbis **56** ©Mike Powell/Getty Images **58** *(sweater)* ©Karina Bakalyan/Shutterstock; *(skirt)* ©Ruslan Kudrin/Shutterstock; *(jeans)* ©Karkas/Shutterstock *(all others)* ©Cambridge University Press **60** ©George Kerrigan **64** *(clockwise from top left)* ©Belinda Images/SuperStock; ©Ingram Publishing/SuperStock; ©Blend Images/SuperStock; ©Punchstock *(mouse)* ©urfin/Shutterstock **66** *(top row, left to right)* ©Catherine Karnow/Corbis; ©Shawn Baldwin/EPA/Newscom; ©Fotosonline/Alamy *(middle row, left to right)* ©Peter Willi/SuperStock; ©Douglas Pulsipher/Alamy; ©KSTFoto/Alamy (bottom row, left to right) ©Cambridge University Press; ©Prisma Bildagentur AG/Alamy; ©S.T. Yiap Still Life/Alamy **67** (top to bottom) ©Bob Krist/Corbis; ©Ron Erwin/Getty Images; ©Bert Hoferichter/Alamy **68** *(clockwise from top left)* ©Enzo/agefotostock; ©Olga Lyubkina/Shutterstock; ©Olga Miltsova/Shutterstock; ©Joseph Dilag/Shutterstock **69** ©Steve Hix/Somos Images/Corbis **71** *(top to bottom)* ©Laura Coles/Getty Images; ©Datacraft Co Ltd/Getty Images; ©panda3800/Shutterstock **72** *(top to bottom)* ©Stephen Johnson/Getty Images; ©Simon DesRochers/Masterfile; ©ImagesEurope/Alamy; ©David Robinson/Snap2000 Images/Alamy75 © Best View Stock/Alamy **76** ©Thinkstock **82** ©Thinkstock **84** *(top to bottom)* ©Exactostock/SuperStock; ©Joe McBride/Getty Images **85** ©David Young-Wolff/PhotoEdit **87** ©Blend Images/SuperStock **90** *(clockwise from top left)* ©Cambridge University Press; ©Alexander Raths/Shutterstock; ©Cambridge University Press; ©Africa Studio/Shutterstock; ©Cambridge University Press; ©Cambridge University Press; ©Cambridge University Press; ©Cambridge University Press; ©Cambridge University Press; ©Lepas/Shutterstock; ©Luis Carlos Jimenez del rio/Shutterstock; ©Jonelle Weaver/Getty Images; ©Cambridge University Press; ©Tetra Images/SuperStock; ©Cambridge University Press; ©Nixx Photography/Shutterstock; ©Orange Stock Photo Production Inc./Alamy; ©simpleman/Shutterstock **91** ©jet/Shutterstock **92**(top row, left to right) ©Cambridge University Press; ©Cambridge University Press; ©Cambridge University Press; ©Thinkstock; ©Cambridge University Press *(top middle row, left to right)* ©Ryan McVay/Thinkstock; ©Valentyn Volkov/Shutterstock; ©Thinkstock; ©Cambridge University Press; ©Cambridge University Press *(bottom middle row, left to right)* ©Cambridge University Press; ©Cambridge University Press; ©Cambridge University Press; ©Cambridge University Press; ©Multiart/Shutterstock (bottom row, left to right) ©Cambridge University Press; ©Cambridge University Press; ©Cambridge University Press; ©Cambridge University Press; ©svry/Shutterstock **93** *(top to bottom)* ©Cambridge University Press; ©Thinkstock; ©Thinkstock; ©Fuse/Getty Images/RF **96** ©Lena Pantiukh/Shutterstock

Text credits

While every effort has been made, it has not always been possible to identify the sources of all the material used, or to trace all copyright holders. If any omissions are brought to our notice, we will be happy to include the appropriate acknowledgements on reprinting.

Special thanks to Kerry S. Vrabel for his editorial contributions.

The top 500 spoken words

This is a list of the top 500 words in spoken North American English. It is based on a sample of four and a half million words of conversation from the Cambridge International Corpus. The most frequent word, *I*, is at the top of the list.

1. I
2. and
3. the
4. you
5. uh
6. to
7. a
8. that
9. it
10. of
11. yeah
12. know
13. in
14. like
15. they
16. have
17. so
18. was
19. but
20. is
21. it's
22. we
23. huh
24. just
25. oh
26. do
27. don't
28. that's
29. well
30. for
31. what
32. on
33. think
34. right
35. not
36. um
37. or
38. my
39. be
40. really
41. with
42. he
43. one
44. are
45. this
46. there
47. I'm
48. all
49. if
50. no
51. get
52. about
53. at
54. out
55. had
56. then
57. because
58. go
59. up
60. she
61. when
62. them
63. can
64. would
65. as
66. me
67. mean
68. some
69. good
70. got
71. OK
72. people
73. now
74. going
75. were
76. lot
77. your
78. time
79. see
80. how
81. they're
82. kind
83. here
84. from
85. did
86. something
87. too
88. more
89. very
90. want
91. little
92. been
93. things
94. an
95. you're
96. said
97. there's
98. I've
99. much
100. where
101. two
102. thing
103. her
104. didn't
105. other
106. say
107. back
108. could
109. their
110. our
111. guess
112. yes
113. way
114. has
115. down
116. we're
117. any

118. he's
119. work
120. take
121. even
122. those
123. over
124. probably
125. him
126. who
127. put
128. years
129. sure
130. can't
131. pretty
132. gonna
133. stuff
134. come
135. these
136. by
137. into
138. went
139. make
140. than
141. year
142. three
143. which
144. home
145. will
146. nice
147. never
148. only
149. his
150. doing
151. cause
152. off
153. I'll
154. maybe
155. real
156. why
157. big
158. actually
159. she's
160. day
161. five
162. always
163. school
164. look
165. still
166. around
167. anything
168. kids
169. first
170. does
171. need
172. us
173. should
174. talking
175. last
176. thought
177. doesn't
178. different
179. money
180. long
181. used
182. getting
183. same
184. four
185. every
186. new
187. everything
188. many
189. before
190. though
191. most
192. tell
193. being
194. bit
195. house
196. also
197. use
198. through
199. feel
200. course
201. what's
202. old
203. done
204. sort
205. great
206. bad
207. we've
208. another
209. car
210. true
211. whole
212. whatever
213. twenty
214. after
215. ever
216. find
217. care
218. better
219. hard
220. haven't
221. trying
222. give
223. I'd
224. problem
225. else
226. remember
227. might
228. again
229. pay
230. try
231. place
232. part
233. let
234. keep
235. children
236. anyway
237. came
238. six
239. family
240. wasn't
241. talk
242. made
243. hundred
244. night
245. call
246. saying

247. dollars
248. live
249. away
250. either
251. read
252. having
253. far
254. watch
255. week
256. mhm
257. quite
258. enough
259. next
260. couple
261. own
262. wouldn't
263. ten
264. interesting
265. am
266. sometimes
267. bye
268. seems
269. heard
270. goes
271. called
272. point
273. ago
274. while
275. fact
276. once
277. seen
278. wanted
279. isn't
280. start
281. high
282. somebody
283. let's
284. times
285. guy
286. area
287. fun
288. they've
289. you've
290. started
291. job
292. says
293. play
294. usually
295. wow
296. exactly
297. took
298. few
299. child
300. thirty
301. buy
302. person
303. working
304. half
305. looking
306. someone
307. coming
308. eight
309. love
310. everybody
311. able
312. we'll
313. life
314. may
315. both
316. type
317. end
318. least
319. told
320. saw
321. college
322. ones
323. almost
324. since
325. days
326. couldn't
327. gets
328. guys
329. god
330. country
331. wait
332. yet
333. believe
334. thinking
335. funny
336. state
337. until
338. husband
339. idea
340. name
341. seven
342. together
343. each
344. hear
345. help
346. nothing
347. parents
348. room
349. today
350. makes
351. stay
352. mom
353. sounds
354. change
355. understand
356. such
357. gone
358. system
359. comes
360. thank
361. show
362. thousand
363. left
364. friends
365. class
366. already
367. eat
368. small
369. boy
370. paper
371. world
372. best
373. water
374. myself
375. run

376. they'll
377. won't
378. movie
379. cool
380. news
381. number
382. man
383. basically
384. nine
385. enjoy
386. bought
387. whether
388. especially
389. taking
390. sit
391. book
392. fifty
393. months
394. women
395. month
396. found
397. side
398. food
399. looks
400. summer
401. hmm
402. fine
403. hey
404. student
405. agree
406. mother
407. problems
408. city
409. second
410. definitely
411. spend
412. happened
413. hours
414. war
415. matter
416. supposed
417. worked
418. company
419. friend
420. set
421. minutes
422. morning
423. between
424. music
425. close
426. leave
427. wife
428. knew
429. pick
430. important
431. ask
432. hour
433. deal
434. mine
435. reason
436. credit
437. dog
438. group
439. turn
440. making
441. American
442. weeks
443. certain
444. less
445. must
446. dad
447. during
448. lived
449. forty
450. air
451. government
452. eighty
453. wonderful
454. seem
455. wrong
456. young
457. places
458. girl
459. happen
460. sorry
461. living
462. drive
463. outside
464. bring
465. easy
466. stop
467. percent
468. hand
469. gosh
470. top
471. cut
472. computer
473. tried
474. gotten
475. mind
476. business
477. anybody
478. takes
479. aren't
480. question
481. rather
482. twelve
483. phone
484. program
485. without
486. moved
487. gave
488. yep
489. case
490. looked
491. certainly
492. talked
493. beautiful
494. card
495. walk
496. married
497. anymore
498. you'll
499. middle
500. tax